Flying

Donald Crews

Greenwillow Books, New York

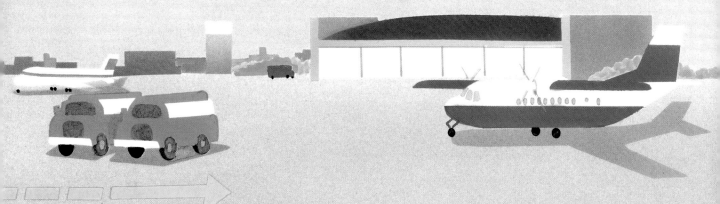

Flying
Copyright © 1986
by Donald Crews
All rights reserved.
Manufactured in China

www.harperchildrens.com
First Edition
10 9 8 7 6

Library of Congress
Cataloging-in-Publication Data
Crews, Donald.
Flying.
"Greenwillow Books."
Summary: An airplane
takes off, flies, and
lands after having passed
over cities, country areas,
mountains, and more.
1. Flight—Juvenile literature.
[1. Flight. 2. Airplanes]
I. Title.
TL547.C68 1986 629.13
85-27022
ISBN 0-688-04318-6 (trade)
ISBN 0-688-04319-4 (lib. bdg.)
ISBN 0-688-09235-7 (pbk.)

Gouache paints and an airbrush
were used for the full-color art.
The typeface is Helvetica Black
Italic.

For those
who make
my heart
soar.

Boarding.

Taxiing to the runway.

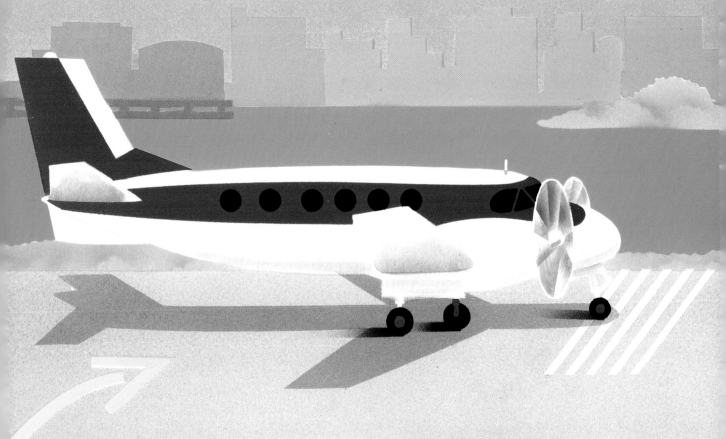

Ready.

Take off.

Flying over the airport.

Flying over the highways.

Flying over rivers.

Flying over cities.

Flying across the country.

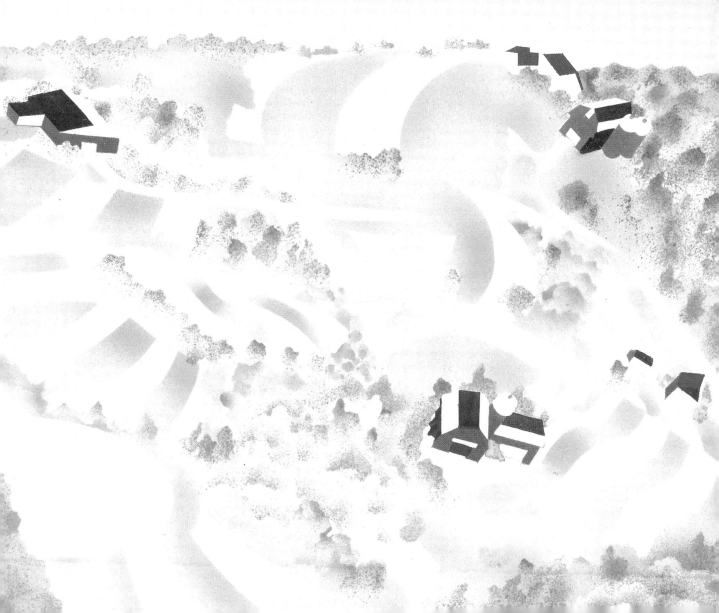

Flying
high over
mountains.

Flying into the clouds.

Flying over the clouds.

Time to head down.

There's
the
airport.

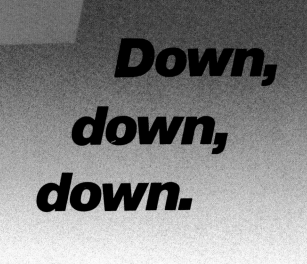

**Down,
down,
down.**

DOWN!